MIKE HARDING is well known as a stan   id-
caster and documentary maker. He fir   he
hitched around the country heading ul.   ran
Islands.

Instilled with a love of the country by his Irish-Catholic family in Mancnester, his love of Ireland was further deepened by one of his teachers at St Bede's College, Manchester – Father Augustus Reynolds. Under his guidance the poetry of Yeats and the plays and writings of J. M Synge took the young poet by the scruff of the neck and sent him reeling onto the Liverpool boat standing with a sunburned thumb at the side of the long road west.

Over the following years he returned to Ireland many times, cycling and walking, playing his banjo in sessions and writing; one result of his wanderings was the acclaimed travel and walking book *Footloose in the West of Ireland,* published by Michael Joseph.

He presented Folk, Roots and Acoustic Music on BBC Radio Two from 1998 to 2012, and now presents a weekly folk show on the internet at www.mike hardingfolkshow.com. He tours extensively with his unique mix of comedy and music, and his shows regularly sell out.

The Connemara Cantos

MIKE HARDING

Luath Press Limited
EDINBURGH
www.luath.co.uk

First Published 2013

ISBN: 978-1-908373-96-0

Typeset in 11 point Sabon
by 3btype.com

Contents

Foreword

I FIRST MET Mike Harding in 1966. Straightaway I realised his love for and his knowledge of Ireland. For 50 years now he has been going deep into the loam. Travelling about the Island Mike listens and observes, converses and shares. He values aspects of Ireland that many of us take for granted. Mike looks behind the walls, gets into the words and music. These poems were written at the hearth, were written from the heart. They stay with me.

Christy Moore

THE CONNEMARA CANTOS

City of Smoke and Stars

Half a life ago I came far west as you could travel,
To a place where turf smoke skeined the air
And the sea wind scattered gulls, raddled
Them like rags all over the Galway sky.

Grey stone city with your arches and your dark haired girls,
Your gargoyles and your mermaids, all this way
For a bucketful of love and an old tinwhistle full of dreams.
The salt-sea wind shook Shop Street and

Hutched in a door a drunk box player busked,
Shawled biddies scuttled by with old string bags,
As the first stars lamped the velvet black
Above you Galway Bay. And here I come once more, back

Here half a century on with my bucketful of words,
Threading beads of verse upon the salty Connemara wind.

The High Stool Hornpipe

Inspired by a tune of the same name written by the artist and composer, Joe Boske.

High on the pub's high stool the poet sits,
Drowning poems by the pint, supping stanzas,
Iambic pentameters of Guinness, trochees of malt,
Spondees of lager chased down with sips of assonance.

Tomorrow, after the black stool and the fry
He will search his pockets for the sonnets he has swilled;
    As much use look for the leaves that fell last year,
Or go looking for the wind out in the field.

And on the next high stool the high painter waits,
Half snoozing, downing noggins of still lives, boozing
Barrels of landscapes, firkins of portraits,
Balloons of abstraction, surreal schooners.

In the morning, with the head Monsignor Bushmills
Has given him, he will scour blank canvases
For the the visions he has supped
    As much use look for the steam from off his piss
In last night's Connemara air as agog he ogled
The Northern Lights, shimmying like his sister Kate.

On the last high stool the piper stares
In real time at his mirrored echo,
Drinking down, jig-time, the crotchets and the quavers;
Drowning crans and rolls, whole reels
And hornpipes, washed down slithering with the slides
And slip jigs down his maw, as the moon glides,
Between the jigs and the reels, over the horns of the bay.

Next day, in the morning's katzenjammer,
When the cats are jamming at
The dustbin's feline fleadhceol,
He will search the leaden silence for the music he has lost.
    As much use look for the half-set he has left
Together with his jacket and his fags under the high stool.

There the cleaner of the morning with her brush
Will find the dotted crotchets of un-fingered, stillborn tunes
All coated with the gentle, harmless, dust
Of jumbled, fractured, crumpled words,
The cracked and peeling pigments of lost visions.

As she picks up the pipes she hears a noise
And peers and looks, then bending down,
Ear close, she listens; and the finely dwindling dust
Is lilting in a small and fading voice, reel-time,
'We could have been – we could have been – we could have been...'

Einstein And The Inishbofin Cow

*'What is the stars Joxer? What is the stars?' Sean O' Casey – Juno
and the Paycock*

I stumbled from the house one night,
Half-drunk, be-fuddled, binoculars in hand,
And lay spread eagled in the haggard staring up
Into a Connemara sky addled with stars.
In the bay the tide was grumbling on the strand;
There was a touch of frost, untramelled air,
I was a lone soul in an indigo bowl
Spattered with long spilt milk
That nobody was crying over.

They say the witch of Inishbofin stripped
The magic cow into a colander,
Until, heart broke, it hoofed
And kicked the bucket spattering
The black night sky with a froth of stars,
And so the Milky Way was born.

I raised the glasses to my eyes and then,
With Joxer, Captain Boyle and Einstein
At my shoulder, turned the knurled wheel
And, as the spatterings crystalised, I fell
Not down but up, starwards into the reeling sky,
Tumbling, assumed, like Alice in reverse to Heaven.

Star beyond star beyond star beyond star,
The dust of eternity flew past,
Spangles of light, shimmering motes –
Each one a star, a galaxy, countless,
Confounding understanding. So
I followed the White Rabbit deeper up
Than I had ever been, out and beyond
And on to where no time at all began.
And in this star-lit haggard, humped
In stony Connemara uphill from Cleggan bay;
On this island, on this spinning ball of rock;
In this solar merry-go-round,
This galaxy, this Cosmos, this Creation
On this Connemara night –
The sea a distant rumour on the strand –
I heard the whispering of a million gods
And fairies, djins and pookhas, seraphim
And cherubim, sun-breathing dragons,
Tail-swallowing snakes, Balor
Kali and Buddha, Crom Dubh, Vishnu and Allah,
Yaweh, Bridgid, Ganesha and Christ
Moving out across the singing universe.

And I sensed the unfathomable mystery of it all
This blue-green ball, this howling, turning lump
Of matter and of men roiling through Time,
And I felt myself sucked up and out into the void,
Knowing nothing – only that there were,
At that same moment, alchemists at work
In the Hall of the Mountain Kings.
In a cave carved out of the eternal rock
Deep down in the land of the cuckoo clock
A tribe of Branestawms were picking at the lock
Of the Cosmos with an inch of soggy string.

And aiding and abetting them were Captain Boyle,
The table rappers and Sir Conan Doyle,
Archie and Mehitabel and Old Malarkey
The Mad Hatter, Old Moore and Bishop Berkley,
Chicken Licken, Mother Shipton and Nostradamus,
Einstein, Biddy Early and old Confucius,
Who confused as us were trying to count
The dancing angels on the pins bright head.
They were searching for the Quarks, hunting out the Snarks,
The Will o' the Whisps, the Jacks in the Mist,
The photons, the protons, the old Puck Fair Goatons,
The Alchemists' Stone, (and wouldn't you know son,
They were even hunting the old Higgs Boson)
Constraining to construct another narrative
As real as Juno, Joxer and the Inishbofin cow.
Dish, spoon, cow, moon;
Stars, Mars, too many jars.

Permit this tipsy tap-room Aristotle to unbottle –
For all you Popes, Philosophers and Physicists and drunks –
His Grand Unifying Theory Of The Clarity of Bugger–all:
As Wittgenstein while living at Rosroe along the coast,
Over his spilt milk, his crematorium toast,
After moaning about the midges might have intoned,
'By the Father, Son and the Holy Ghost,
Of what we do not know; of that we must write poems.'

Briste An File

In Donegal, Glencolumbkille
Our little rented cottage stood below the hill,
Looking as if it grew there like a lichen or a moss;
There was the faint rumour of surf upon the strand,
Whispering gossip of the field-away sea;
There was turf smoke, a diddling burn
Haggling over the price of cobbles, and
An old cow mooching in the bohareen.

Miles of mountain tracks had grubbed the duds,
So I washed the pants and hung them out
To dry on the blustering wind, that mad march air
That was using gulls as dusters to polish the Donegal sky.

And that night somebody stole them,
Some unholy swine had offed them:
Briste an file – the poet's pants. All gone.
Lifted by a common criminal of old Gleann Cholm Cille,
The trouserless poet – left with nothing but a curse
Between his backside and the wind – shouted,

'May he hobble through Hell
Backwards with his balls on fire,
For God's life and a half!
May he get the squint and the squitters
The pox, the palsy and the mange,
And may the only callers at his house
Be wanting money or his daughters! Deranged,
Let him see the moon coming out of his arse!
And when all that has passed
May he marry his grandmother,
And may their first child be a cat!'

And at that I noticed them, the purloined pants,
The burgled bags, hung up on the furze above the ditch,
Flapping as though a cartoon ghost was wearing them
Running on the spot – escape arrested; frozen
Where the Hades-hobbling, cat-fathering,
Grandmother-marrying, balls-on-fire,
Moon-arsed, innocent Donegal wind had carried them.

Cairn Makers

Stone on stone, word on word, note on note –
All you can hope for at the close of everything.
As Micho Russell said, 'Don't get too clever
Or it'll all be nothing but a bottle of old smoke.'

Inch on inch the tides come, and inch on inch they go,
Moons span the line from headland to the hills,
Day follows day and all that you can hope
Is that, when all the mourners go their way, still

Your small cairn of simple stuff will stand. Cairns mark the way
On and off the hill. Those stone fists bunched
On the crags black rim have their narrative, they say,
'I too came this way, and this is what I did

In my small time here, my long time gone.'
And this is all we can any hope to do:
To leave our own small marker on the great fell of the world –
Note on note, stone on stone, word on word.

The Rain Would Drive You To Drink

Not just the rain: wind, fog, mist and snow,
Cold, sleet, ice, frost, thunder,
Lightning (sheet, ball and fork)
But most especially strangely – sometimes sunshine.

Opening a bar door on a brass-bright, summer's day
Looking for Joe, I see only lurkers on high stools.
Like heifers in a winter stall they stare at me,
A silhouette framed in a furnace door,
Then turn back to the matter between their hands,
Snug in their smoky underworld. Old days
The fairy music drew men under hills
Or into fairy forts, bewitched,
And sent them gibbering home with tunes to play
And tales to tell. But now the wide screen and
The Lotto seem to serve as well.

But the rain set in the rot,
The everlasting, whooring, forty shades of rain,
And the colonising boot,
That never lets up, even on this long midsummer day,
Of the grey Atlantic skies
That have kicked this sodden July all to hell.
The Inuit, they say, have forty words for snow.
The Irish should have a hundred words at least
For rain.

A soft day and the dark come early
Sucking all the colour from the land.
The harbour lamps come sputtering on,
I drive along to Joe's and see in the half-light,
Courting the ditch, a staggering man.
Head down and coatless in the mithering rain,
He walks like a sick calf, no thought but for home.
And there: a wife, the TV on, his dinner dry
And covered with a plate, and kids ready to fly
His bottle-fed rage his windmill fists.

He lurches, teeters on the ditch's edge,
Dances, spins then lifts
His head and curses come
On God, the rain, the bogs
And the horse that fell this afternoon at Doncaster.
The maledictions rattle his teeth,
Raging like comets from his open maw,
Spluttering out across a Connemara summer sky
The colour of a dead nun.

Black Roses

A matter of fact sort of day I don't recall
The weather or the light we had at all.
It was grey I think, we were filming in Tralee
And, when we heard the early morning news, we

Backed the cars against the wall,
Sensing threats that perhaps weren't there at all.
And covered up the British number plates.
For Bobby Sands had just died in the Kesh. That day

We filmed on, the air crackling with hurt and anger.
Then one by one we saw them fluttering, flanking
Every Tralee street until, by the dying of the day, a host
Of black bin liners hung from every pole and post.

Black roses everywhere were blossoming for Roisin Dubh all
Flapping, caioning on a cold, rain-coming, Atlantic squall.

Galway – Dublin Bus 1997

A winter afternoon, grey gales and rain
Scudding the bus on eastwards through
Pinched places with small names,
Where buffeted people, heads down, blew

Along wide streets of empty market towns.
The midlands rolled for ever; rain and wind
Lashed them, smudged and smeared them down
The drab canvas of the road to Dublin. Then we drew in

To somewhere small and dull, with several pubs,
An Oifig an Phoist a news shop with its Lotto,
And a grotto with a Virgin in need of a good rub
And a lick of paint. My head rested on the window,

Half asleep. Then something caught my eye, and I looked up
To see a hand draw back the upstairs curtain lace
And someone in the gap stared down at the bus,
And I suddenly read the certain story of that face:

Old parents to be nursed, a fiancé in the States
The letters drying up as surely as her womb.
Now she haunts the church and rises late
To spend her days ghosting from room to room.

A life stitched by the town's relentless hand,
Mocked by each new dawn, and now the face is leeched
And hungry as the stars, as lonely as a bleached
Branch, driftwood on an empty strand.

The bus revved up, and we pulled out
Leaving behind these things: the cloud of our black smoke,
Oifig an Phoist, a grotto, and two virgins staring down
The wintry, rain-washed, darkening Dublin road.

The Builder's Hammer

The builder's hammer is on the roof,
The chippy's plane and saw,
All where they left them when they heard the news,
And rushed in their vans to the shore.

Three days they say and the sea gives up
The dead, but still his mother waits,
And all the sea gives up to this empty bay,
Is old floats, rope, bottles, old crates.

A lad from the townland is lost from his boat
And kept by the begrudging sea,
And a light in the window burns through the dark nights
To call him back home. But he

Stays out where the cold Atlantic waves
Hold him in their iron grey hands,
And each high tide his mother walks the bay
Combing the empty strand.

And the builder's hammer is on the roof,
The chippy's plane and saw,
Still where they left them when, they heard the news,
And rushed in their vans to the shore.

Hands of the Country

As she sat in her old chair staring in the fire
I traced my four year old fingers along the backroads
Of her hands, the valleys between the knuckles,
The soft downlands, the hills of old bone that rose

Over the slack, silk-skinned plains.
I travelled with my soft child's touch
Along the byways of those aged, veined
Hands, following, without knowing it

Lanes that would lead me on through all the years
To my own far country, and with time
To other small soft fingers on my hands
Tracing their way through my own storied lands.

Mountain Barry

I.M. Barry Halpin AKA Lord Lucan. Died Goa, India 2003

'He's home in Glasstown from that Indian beach.'
The words would go out over the Guinness and the smoke,
Three fingers of malt and the barmaid's reach.
A mythology of Barrys rose: he was the bloke

Who played the banjo all round Europe, climbed
The Idwall Slabs alone half-pissed; who filled
His sister's hall with chiming pyramids
Of empty bottles when he came home from his trips.

Australia, India, Africa, Japan; the bars and streets
Of most towns in this world had known his sweet
Wild music. 'He could get,' they said, 'a tune
From a potato.' Tin sandwich, banjo, flute,

Guitar and concertina, in his hands transmuted air
And wood into the music heard beneath the stones:
Paddy's Rambles In The Park, Boolavogue
Níl An Lá – he would travel days to hear

Good music – Tansey, Casey, Sherlock, Doran they
All knew Mad Mountain Barry.
     He went away
To his last home to die, in Goa beneath the bleached
Ribs of a long-beached boat that was his home now. 'His nibs

Holds court to all the hippies, and young things
Without a stitch on, lives on fags and booze,
His feet haven't known a pair of shoes
Since he left Glasstown last.' One more last trip to sing

And drink and show his liver who was boss,
And then back home to India to gain whatever we had lost.
There was a glimmer of him in the corner of
Some TV documentary, just a flash, then he was gone.

The stories came: the last calm hours, the funeral pyre,
And then the beard and that wild hair were all just smoke, a heat
Haze bending the unreal world of that far beach.
And the notes of jigs and hornpipes songs and reels

And stories, rose in flecks of ash above the mangrove trees
Along that shore, lilting on the air, diddling on the breeze,
Making their way home from Goa to Milltown Malbay
In between the jigs and reels of the Willy Clancy.

Only A Man, In A Boat, On A Lake

Only a man in a boat on a lake,
Sun-washed with evening as the fish
Sip fat, soft sedges in the shallows and
Coots fuss and fret amongst the reeds.

Only a man in a boat on a lake,
The mountains echoed with the salmon clouds
In the still warm lough. No wind troubles the water's
Glass broken only by the subtle bull's eyes of the rising trout.

Only a man in a boat on a lake,
Watching the sun slide over the rim of the world,
His pipe and his rod, and the swans
Who, so silent, sail softly by the reeds.

Only a man in a boat on a lake,
The mountains and the late summer day
Softly fading around him, the first star
Low over the mountains to the south.

Only a man in a boat on a lake,
On the bank a dog fox sees him
And its copper fur, caught by the dying sun,
Becomes a brassy flash arcing a drystone wall.

Only a man in a boat on a lake,
And somewhere else there is a world
Of money and of war, of getting
And of holding; a world apart.

But, here and now, on this small tarn,
In this breath, this pinch of time,
There is, as the stars begin to fleck the sky,
Only a man in a boat on a lake.

Hulme Five – August 1969

1 *The Economics Lesson*

'See, now' said the ganger, 'What it is is this;
Clear as the day, any fool could understand.
You know we're building slums,
I know we're building slums,
The subbies know we're building slums,
The site foreman knows we're building slums,
The clerk of works knows we're building slums,
The quantity surveyors know we're building slums;
The city planners know we're building slums –
Even One Eyed McGuinness with half a brain
And that so pickled in drink he's a fire hazard,
Even he and the Lord mayor and the feckin',
Lord Mayor's cat and the mouse it's chasing
Know we're building slums –
Even Nelly who makes the bacon butties in the canteen
Knows we're building slums!

But it's economics see.
There's so much money swirling round the pot,
So many fingers in the pie, necks on the block,
More bloody fiddles than Hey Diddle Diddle.
Like a steam roller going downhill out of control
With Shit for Brains Murphy at the wheel
There's balls-all anyone can do to stop the game;
The man who made the decision's probably dead
Or pissed off or in hiding – all the same.

In thirty years we'll be knocking the bastard down
More jobs then for Paddy in old Manchester town.
Now drink your tea and stop your chunterin';
And get on with that bloody concrete shutterin'.'

2   *The Irish Club*

Porter black as a curate's cassock topped
With a head of creamy, soft Croagh Patrick clouds;
Smoke and laughter spool the room
While in the corner, calling the tune,
Are piper, fiddle and squeeze box.
Then a waltz is crooned and the dark night is
Set back and tinkers and Kerrymen lilt along.

For some the far green hills of Sligo and the bare
Stone teeth of Connemara come too close, and eyes
Glazed with salt tears see the mirrored glass and wood bar blur,
And the spinning couples sliding past,
Are smeared as in a mountain mist and the room
Grows soft as veils of sea fret come sweeping in
From out so well remembered bays
And the hills of Connemara come too close.

3 On The Lump

A lorry drops him off at the end of day,
Soil and sweat on Friday's suit, his boots clay-
Clagged. In his one-bar, one-bulb
Room he has a swill, then heads out for the pub,

A sixpenny bus ride down to High Stool Hall;
Mahogany, etched glass, the warmth, the craic,
The schooners that turn time around, blunt pain, so that
Mayo's whispering ghost recedes beyond the city's pall.

But the lips of the women are not for him,
The breasts of the women are not for him,
The smiles of the women are not for him.
The love of the women is not for him.

No warm back to spoon into, only
Cold, soiled sheets, in a damp, rank room
That reeks of piss and loneliness. But a lagoon
Of stout would not put out
The desert thirst of this bold navvy man,
Nor a universe of moons light up his dark.
And so he's out again – a whistle from a far-off train,
A bark from a somewhere dog – buying painted smiles
From shivering girls; love by the pound in Hanky Panky Park.
'Come on Paddy – I'll show you a good time.'

And the same full moon scuds through the broken cloud
Above the Salford alley where the bargain's struck,
The same old moon that limes Croagh Patrick, and shines down
Upon the wind-ragged streets of Kiltimagh.

4 *Tiny O' Reiley's Dream*

'Well bolloxed' said Tiny o' Reiley to his beer
'Sure the bonus is well bolloxed' As we supped
Our Guiness in the warm, smoke-softened snug.
'The bonus sure is bolloxed and the whole job is well bolloxed!
I'd be back in Merrion Square if I'd only got the fare
And tearin' up the lino in O' Donaghues.'

But we both well knew that old Monsignor Booze
Meant Dublin wouldn't see his arse for many a year.
The ticket money in his Friday hand
Was cold piss drying on the wall by Monday clocking on.

Nameless navvies on the lump,
Digging ditches, humping bricks,
Building brave new slums for old.
Already the walls were glazed with water, and the rats
And roaches had moved in with pac a macs
And wellies, one step-dance ahead
Of the hangman's wonderful daughter.
'Friday the Golden Eagle shits !' said Tiny O' Reiley
'I'll be down The Exile of Erin with the box
And bollox to them all is the Wild O' Reiley's call!'

But Tiny's playing hornpipes for the angels now;
A careless hammer dropped from ten floors up
Parted his hair and then his head
On a high-rise scheme somewhere in Birmingham.
There was an empty seat on the Friday Dublin boat
From Holyhead, the priest carried a message
Up a cow-raddled old farm lane,
Oxfam got three pairs of built up shoes,
And the lino's safe still in O'Donaghues.

5   *Paddy No One*

Noone he writes, one night, tongue out, as No one
For a laugh in Longsight, on a split beer mat
With a betting shop pen. 'Noone –
It's No one – the name – you know.' But

No one sees Paddy Noone shadowed below
In the shuttering, taking a leak amongst
The web of steel; the bucket swings and Casey from Carlow
Concretes him in. No sound, no shout, no one

So much as misses Noone. A navvy on the lump,
No records kept, no questions asked;
They think he's jacked, has slung
His hook for a better rate on the new by-pass.

The woman at the digs bins his rosary, his few soiled clothes,
And a wife on a western island watches down the road,
And tells the children there'll be letters soon
From Manchester, from Daddy No one, Paddy Noone.

The Irish For Oasis

Crossing the badlands of North London
On a Sunday summertime, they go
By griddle pavements and brick terrace ovens
To the Favourite in Holloway Road.

After-mass caravans of baggy-suited men; rolled
In their jacket pockets, truncheoned Irish Posts.
Pints in the dark room, and Sweet Afton smoke
Whorls in the window light, spools, coils.

Martin the fiddler gives a nod, the squeeze-box wheezes
Out a chord, and then they jig it out: Hitler's Downfall.
Men move like palm trees in a cooling breeze,
This pub a haven in a burning, dry, dust bowl.

And, in the deserts beyond this small oasis,
This Kalahari of yellow brick streets.
Is the smell of English beef and Sunday roasts
As London jigs and twitches in the heat.

July Barbers

From Mayo, God help us, each summer they came
And stood to be hired in Salt Kettle Lane,
And the farmers would pass with a swagger and a nod,
A hand slap, a wink, the chink of a few bob,
To drink 'your man's health' – and the bargain was struck
Binding them to the land. The truck
Picked them up when the pubs had all shut
And tipped them, tipsy and singing,
Into the lamplit yard, their beery breath
Wreathing round the moth-danced flame.
Then it was weeks of aching days of
Scything, raking, turning, loading,
Footcocks, jockeys, cart and barn,
Sun-up to the edge of light;
Then blood spilled, ran, and filled the sky,
And men grew field-long stalking shadows.

Sleeping on straw they rose first light, swilling the night
Out of their eyes at the trough, washing
The gall of loneliness from their mouths,
The smell of bacon fingering the air
As mist smudged a heron on the river and a curlew
Bubbled at the orange ball that rimmed the fell.
Sunday, sixteen miles to mass, on foot,
And sixteen back, then a few pints and the craic,
Three hours of bed and another rising – 'God bless the work!'
Some nights they sang in Irish beneath a shaking moon,

Moving through the watery light
Over a lime-lit land fecund with seed and fruit.

They combed the hayfield mowing to the lilt
Of an old song and called God's blessing on
The field's pan-scrub chin, well razored.
'Tis a shave will last all year mister!'
Later, from the barn the farmer heard
The soft murmur of Gaelic chanting,
'Like bloody Ju-Ju it sounded, Methody ranting.'
Peering through a crack he saw them kneeling
Haloed in the lamplight, as horny fingers,
Scythe-segged, told the Rosary through
Their voices chanted, the beads crackled,
And Pen-y-Ghent became Crough Patrick.

Family Album

Only now my faltering voice can give
A stuttering pale echo to
Their stories; only now
Can I begin transmuting all their tales

Into my own. Now I translate
The daysongs of their lives
One story for a thousand winter's nights
Fireside words hugging the hearth.

The burden of the tale commands the hearer
In this whispering Chinese chain of links and rings
To carry on the narrative. And so it goes
The albatross necklace swings

As the ship sloughs, sluices down the cusp
Of the wave towards King Cotton and his city
The slum streets and the rack of labour, lint and dust.
Love is so sore, there is no pity.

One constant recitative runs through all their lives,
'Hands-work, pay-day, bees in a hive.'
Leaving behind landlords and begrudgery
To scratch a living from the iron face of drudgery.

Leaving the North Wall

In the half tones of the dawn
The running cattle caoining and wall eyed
Hoofs clabbering on the cobbles,
Horns lunging, slaver stringing
As they were loaded up the shit-caked ramp,
You stood, each one with your small bundles,
Cardboard suitcase, half a handful
Of you, herded. 'Country people.' the gardai said
Dismissively and the gangway sucked you up
And ferried you away in the grey dead light.

Once out beyond the point and the nodding buoys,
The Sugar Loaf diminishing,
The coast a rumor of grey green,
The great whale of the ship bucked towards
Liverpool, leaving behind it in a trail
Of hissing foam melting into the mist,
The whispered images of your people's past:

The railway station and the waking crowd,
The shy hand-clasping at the Parting Bridge,
The chip of stone from the hearth, the bottle
Of water from the well, the cob
Of turf from off the reek, and fields of
Stubble, hay time ending with the neighbors
Straightening up and waving as they gathered in
The gleanings. All of this hissing

In the wake that feathers out into the mist,
Bubbling silver becoming swelling lead,
The cattle boats butting, blunt, iron snout
Rutting blindly towards the foreign years ahead.

Makers Of Magic, Carriers Of Light

Oh you makers of magic, oh you carriers of light:
Arms full of brightness and truth.

By the fire on a winter's night,
Stories and songs and music,
Shadow animals handmade on a wall:
Dogs and swans and cheeping birds,
All made simply for the making.

Out in the fields on a mad March day,
Scribbling stories on the sky with fists
Full of rooks and branches,
Setting words and song free
Watching where the knowing dances.

Oh you tellers of stories, unlocked from who knows where,
You midnight dancers on the whistling ice,
You painters opening windows on the world,
You potters breathing clay to life
Oh you bringers of magic, oh you tellers of tales,
You makers of music, you carriers of songs
Sung for the empty and the lost.

Out there the gimcrack world bangs on
It's tacky kettles, and pulls on it's shoddy cloths
Hiding behind its daubs, its counterfeit colours,
Its petty gimcrack tunes, its whore words
Weasling their way, slithering across the mud.

And the makers in the still, quiet rooms
Open starburst windows in the clouds,
Paint rainbow birds on trees that never were,
Grab fistfuls of bright stars,
And scatter them. about the night,
Send music leaping in bright showers,
Small children dancing, the old sat nodding
By the open door through which they just make out
The ever beckoning hand.

And all the stories and the songs
The pictures and the plays
The music and the dance are the pure drop
The true philosophers stone. And it is done
Not for the money or the fame,
But for that brief few moments when you cup it in your hands:
That bright, mysterious, elusive flame
The aisling geal, that lights the world and cheers the dark
And you carry it before you tenderly,
An infinitely precious thing.
Oh you makers of magic, oh you carriers of light.

The Man To Write The Book

I knew him only by his workday name,
'Paddy,' his bullet head aflame
With the copper turnings of tight curls.
Six foot and some, hands like two brickie's hods,
He would dig all day furling the sod
In easy natural grace as though the hard, red clay,
The northern English footings,
Were the soft skin of a Connemara bog;
His shovel sinking like a knife in cream.
A hundredweight bag of cement rode on
Each shoulder, hit the back of the mixer with a crack.

One morning in the hut, 'You'll be the man,' he said,
'To write the book.' We shared
Small knowledge but large understanding
On that bleak site down in the smoky town
In a valley once, 'the most beautiful in all
Of England.' Now it was a red brick canyon choking
On the bile of it's own black and bitter smoke.
The river once so full of trout and salmon you could walk
Across their backs from bank to bank now rank with rats
And foamed man-high with the shit the money men
Poured in.
    And there was me and Paddy, our covenant
As tacit as a wink and nod,
He to the shovel I to the hod;
The college boy – the Sunshine Navvy,

And the Connemara man, no name but Paddy.
Come term time I'd the ticket out
And I'd be carrying books instead of bricks
The only concrete – nouns, the only sub – a clause;
His ticket only went, it seemed, one way.

The day after I got my cards and left
They said Paddy, as though bereft,
Had scattered the chairs and tables in the hut
Like autumn leaves, his eyes wide open shut,
Raging, six to hold him down.
'No reason.' they all said,
'He just did one. He just kicked off!' And I can see
You, Paddy, in my mind, lashing at the cruel chains of air,
The money manacles, the pay-day Friday cuffs,
Bright eyes fixed on an unreachable horizon,
The smell of seaweed off the rocks,
Salt on your tongue, wind in your copper hair,
And the far off fins of wine-red hooker sails
In a shining, mackerel coloured Connemara bay.

THE CONNEMARA CANTOS

Moone The Poet

'Moone the Poet' it shouted out across the world
From the poster in the window of the best hotel in town.
And the precious poet, state of the hearts,
Arts week -primed, versified and rhymed
Before the stanza-starved and haiku-hungry crowd.

Outside the west of Ireland got on with
It's non-poetry, non-festival, non-arts week way:
Women with late shopping, a farmer with a sick
Calf in a trailer. and four sweating, swearing men
Maneuvering a particularly heavy piece
Of furniture across the busy street.

'Moone the Poet.' Perhaps seeing it as a command
Four small, bold boys, pulling down their pants,
Pressed their little bottoms on the lower panes
And royally mooned the poet Moone,
Who, back to the well framed bums, was wallowing
Deep in the slough of his own angst,
And wondered why he was telling the sorry tale
Of his nineteenth nervous breakdown
To a rocking, sweating, snorting, giggling room
That had seen a noonday, rising Connemara moon.

Running Backwards on the Beach at Glassilaun

The long strand on this August day is empty but for us,
The waves slow roll at the tide's turning almost hushed
In the hum of summer and you, the runner, now near eighty
Are trotting backwards from your small grandchild,
Who totters after you along the singing sand.
I have that picture locked into my very soul:
That day, your family and you, your laughter loud
Above the murmuring sea, the shimmering sky,
The picnic blankets the bright beach ball and you,
Our mother, running backwards on the beach at Glassilaun.

Now, the funeral done, I see you running
Backwards down the telescope of time
And I cannot bring you back no matter how
I try. I watch you go until you are a far off speck,
With your spider shadow skittering beside you on
The shining sands, and Mweelrea a looming bulk behind.
And you are running backwards on the beach at Glassilaun,
And in my mind's eye running backwards to your past.

I see you – what? Sixteen or seventeen years old?
A young girl at the bright door of the days to come:
The bombing and the years of war,
The burning cities and the Earth groaning
With the numberless and nameless dead. I see
The long song of your struggles and your joys

Your children and grandchildren,
And your slide into the silent, darkening land
A land where only you could go
And only you could speak the language:
Erewhon, Hi Brasil, Cockayne;
Elusive, shifting always out of reach –
You were the queen of that strange country.

And you are running backwards on the beach at Glassilaun,
And we can only watch you, we are dumb and cannot call.

Walking Mother To The Car

Years ago you carried me
Straddled on your hip as women do
World over and have always done, my weight
Nothing to you back then. But now
I lead you to the car hung on my arm;
Breath and a bag of sticks is all – for all
The weight of years no heavier, as though
A small dry whitethorn branch has caught
Up on my sleeve, rootless, weightless
Futureless, and I am carrying it along.

Sean Nós Dancer

A shadow from the corner he moves out
And shyly takes the floor, smiling.
Already you can tell just from his stance
His eyes see nothing more, trance dancer.

His hands are held out loose, waist high,
As though he carries a thing infinitely light
And infinitely precious before him, then the feet
Batter the flags and the hands fall. Neat

Small steps, pauses, spins then on he moves,
And the music follows him around the room.
Somehow he has keyed into the infinite
And his slotted steps tread the anger and the bright

Loves, the joys and stories of the tribe.
The music takes him and possesses him
And something secret is brought out,
And the story moves on. Bound and

Whirling with the dance he spirals,
Brushing the gracious delicacy of a boot on stone
Gone beyond he conjures up our dreams
The music stops he comes back to the room

And smiles to whoops and screams
Shyly crossing the bar-room half in a dream
As though he himself only half understands,
A traveller returning from some different, stranger land.

Four Irish Tunes

1 *The Lark On The Strand*

'Singing its heart out.' Once they would have said
But poets now know better and throw words
Like 'heart' and 'love' into the trash; searching instead,
For irony and tone to bring the cure.

Yet here upon the strand – Atlantic combers shrunk
To a lapping on the shore – a speck, a dribble
Of feathers, blood and bone sings out its heart, drunk
With love, writing across this Donegal bay scribbles

Of joy. My soul in shreds I walk
The healing strand, beneath the sky's blue benisons,
And poetry comes like summer snow, blessings
Falling from the throat of a sky-hung lark.

2 *The Maid Behind The Bar*

The lechery and the lager she can handle,
Even the men who take language and mangle
It until it becomes a slither of sounds,
Their banana hands signing the profound
Wisdom and sincerity of the speaker. Cheek and lip
She can deal with, even the landlord's slips
As his hand, aiming (supposedly) for the till,
Brushes her breasts. She pulls the gills
And pints she smiles and works her hours.
Even the women affronted by her youth who glower,

Drinking their past into the future, resenting her
Thick, red-gold hair, her lips edged on a smile, she doesn't mind.

All of this will pass. For they none of them can hear
Her dreams or guess how Krakow stalks
This room; how Poland walks between the tables,
The turf fire, the flat screen; how when she goes
Out for a smoke the stars she sees
Above the yard are not the stars of Connemara
But the stars above the lake before her fathers house.
Where even now, as the guards cruise slowly past the pub,
The cows are breathing softly in their stalls
As her father locks the hens in for the night.
And he too looks up at the stars and sees
Her in her first communion dress, and sees
Her as she was the day she left, the fleeting images
Clutching at his heart like a curious pain.

And he sets the old wooden barrow down,
The rake and shovel against the wall,
And in the woods above this Connemara town
The hunting screech owls call.

3   *Sligo Maid*

Somebody wearing your perfume
Walked past me today, and here
In this dull café room
Stalked suddenly the leopard of love. Away

Went dust and cobwebs the wrappings of care,
Banished misfortune went tripping up the stairs,
Found all the longings and trappings still there
Of nights and days and reeling times shared,

A universe of cool linen
Sheets, after-shower skin,
Pale breasts marbled with blue,
Silk soft thighs, the black triangle
Of wet fur - oh and all the burning
Of those moments' cadenza:

Wind and rain off Sligo,
And a secret shimmering in the West.
And all lost, for ever lost and gone
With the spume that bowls along the shore;
Until stirred in memory's boneyard
By a faint scent singing above the city's roar.

4   *My Darling Asleep*

In this small continent of a room
All history distills itself into the folds
Of stockings cast careless across the chair,
The bra and knickers tumbled to the floor.
And all philosophy is in your form
Sleeping out the summer night,
All art is in the curl of your fingers
Around the pillow's edge.

And I stand at the window
Listening to the sleeping townland,
The world shrunk to a lone dog's bark,
The wind stirring the new leaves on the trees.
And I know now that all religions lie
Here in this room, all knowledge, all
Understanding – here in this small everywhere
All I know is here and even God himself
Is in your every sleeping breath.

Slipway

There is nothing out beyond this last slim spur of land
But the darkness of the gathering night;
Nothing moves out there but the World's old skin
Slackly rising and falling, whispering amongst
The tangled trails of bladderwrack,
Burnishing the barnacled rocks.
They shine, silvered in the cold lights of the dock.

There is nobody – a cat leaping a crate is all.
Nothing, except that far out beyond the bay
There will be sailors leaning on the rail on watch,
Staring at our harbour lights, perhaps,
And looking down at the sussuration of foam
Capping the wash, their heads all bucketful
Of dreams of lovely women and soft beds.

There is nowhere beyond until the blue pack-ice
And fret-work of the coast, the fjords of
Greenland locked in winter half the year.

There is nothing more but the journey,
There is nothing else but the path,
And tonight no boat will come
Clamourous with light and laughter to this shore.

Fluteplayer

In memoriam Bill Sloyan, Kiltimagh, Co Mayo and Cheetham Hill, Manchester.

As down the glen came Mc alpine's men,
Their shovels slung behind them
It was in the pub that they supped their sub
And it's down in the spike you'll find them.

Thick fingers flickering on the keys
Spin notes across the smoky room and caoin
A music made forgotten years ago,
A teem of times in houses in the West.
By lurking bogs you learned the tips and rolls
And trod dark country miles to fill
The reeking harvest barns with tunes
Till the room grew quiet again.
And in the dawn your slow airs lured
The birds down from the trees, and called
The lovers from the roadside ditch.

Here now the room is brassy with the smell of work,
And brick faced men with hands like hods
Breathe malty fireside talk of homes
They'll see no more. While, through it all,
Your eyes tight closed, your bald
Head slightly tenderly bowed, the old
Tunes warm the room: Boy in the Gap,
Tenpenny Bit, Banish Misfortune. And
The bar room moves as a labourer,

Clay-booted and lopsided with his stout,
Tips neatly through the measure of a jig
He last heard at a cross-roads in the West.

They little know the boys back on the site
That a poet and a piper walk their midst.
Tomorrow those same fingers rule a line
Or flick curled shavings from a new planed length,
Feed bright brass screws into the yielding grain
As the lilting of the mixer fills the air.

The Song of the Flute

Blow a breath into me, man; lip to ebony lip
And make the thick air quicken, pulse and thrum.
Tip and swirl the tune, your fingers flickering up
My spine, and let reel around the pub
My throbbing soul of wood. From root to branch,
From core to twig, from heart to wrist to fingers – cran
And roll the music, spin the tune out of the room

Onto the strand where brother wind
Is stroking the soft heads of the waves
And the set dancers on the harbour flags twist
And wind to the tunes tipple and shout. Man chance
A swirl of wood-song, tap-root dance.

Such an small stick in the hollow of your hand
Come, lip to lip and let us, lovers, kiss.

The Old Bog Road, November 2010

You could be on the surface of the moon
But for the water; water everywhere, dark pools
And brackish loughs far as the eye can see;
A filigree of bog-land, furze and peat.

In this limpid, wintry light it seems that silver solder
Has been let flow in every dip and fold.
You stand agog in a land mercurial, nothing but bog
And fen and rock and broom. Waterlogged,

A drowned moon, a hollow land
Where it seems no hand has ever so much as turned
A stone. But wander from the road
A small way you will see, far off, a gable end,

All that is left of what once was a home, now fallen.
Closer by, knee high, all that still stands
Of a cottage wall, all in it long gone now to England
Or the American boats. Within those walls

Once voices called and sang, children
Were born, the old ones died. God knows
Somehow they wrung a living from these fens.
Their story lost, this rubble all there is to show

That once there was a family here; all gone,
All gone, and blown to the four hard winds.
You can still make out a door, a window sill
And little more, is that a fallen lintel?

Here a greener patch, the haggard stands,
Still bright amongst the heather and the furze;
Beyond: the bitter, mocking ridges of the lazy beds.
Bog cotton trembles in the breeze,

No trees break this rolling ocean swell
Of marsh and heather, lough and pool.
But you can smell a cruel wrong here in the air,
And the very wind asks, how could this have been?

This hollow land is singing, set your ear
To that worn, cottage hearthstone – you will hear
The caoining of the years, of stories lost, the long song
Of a people most grievously wronged;

Of fortune for the favoured few, starvation for the rest.
And the exiles in this land of stone and bog,
Had to learn to eat the air and drink the fog,
Or leave the door ajar and take that old road to the west.

Making The Past

And this is how we make the past: I take
My pen, open the book and write
These words, This summer's evening slides away
The sun sinks Inishbofin bound. An Irish Lights

Ship rides at anchor in the bay
Its dinghy puttering ashore, day
Dies and men head for the bars, for Joyce's
Oliver's, the Pier Bar, or Newman's.

And this is how we make the past
We have no choice, I and the day's end and 'Bofin;'
In the offing, the thirsty, shore-bound sailors in their craft,
A black scarab against the westering sun.

All of us in this span of time, our little lives,
Drawn, meshed together by the web's ineluctable lines.

The Ironmonger's Clerk

Some men pity me my bags of nails,
My bolts and pans and bleach,
My screws and paraffin and my plastic pails
My mops and mouse traps and my hammers, each

Separate item on its allotted shelf;
The dusty floor home to bags of grass seed,
Tubs of sheep dip and unruly reels
Of hose. I hold the iron world of myself

Still behind the counter all the day,
Drink a half of stout with a ham sandwich at Doyle's,
Then get back to my latches and my oils
And keep the ledger neat for old man Fay.

In this small town in Ireland I keep watch,
Through the fly-clotted windows at the raspberry-faced
Old farmers from the hills and the lovely girls with
Long black hair and eyes that are not for me,
And I know they mock the Ironmonger's Clerk.

Yet I have a secret and, when night cloaks all the hills,
I leave the seeds and till, and fires start up like jewels
Upon the bog. And I, Will o' the Whisp with rags
And paraffin that I have taken from the shop
Show all the mockers who's the master now.

The Sun Not Rising

John Donne in Connemara. For Pat.

All night the grey Atlantic sky has wept
And blustered like a drunk at closing time,
And boozy squalls and veils of rain have turned
This summer dawn to cold December.

Grey land, grey skies, grey houses;
Grey islands far out to the west
Are drifting in a world that is all slother
Mizzle and mist – and we not bothered smug and snug in bed.

Fall rain, blow squall, come drizzle and bluff storm,
Come damp, come chill, come half-dead day,
Come wind, come gale, come grey, cold dawn;
Come wild white horses racing down the bay.

All bundled warm and spooned we lie,
Making our own soft Connemara sun, our own blue sky.

This Road

The rain was coming sideways and the wind
Had ripped the skin from off the ribs of the day:
Light failing and a sea of bog, the windscreen
Wipers dancing and Glencolumbkille

Out there somewhere in the watery slather.
But where I didn't know: the map I had
As much use as a chocolate tea pot. I was
Alone in a wilderness made infinite by mist,

In a land where they plant stones and harvest rocks.
There appeared a cottage, turf smoke writhing from its stack.
An old man stooped, the stoker with a sack
Across his shoulders filling a creel from off

The reek. I wound the window down, the rain came in,
He stood, his stance a question. 'Where will this road
Take me?' I asked waving desperately towards the moor
I thought was somewhere out there in the mist.
'This road, sir, will take you anywhere you want
To go.' He nodded, hutched the creel and closed the door.

Train By Skerries

The Mourne Mountains a blue crinkle in the haze
Our train flickered by, running a dog along the
Railings its shadow barking after us.
Children on the beach waved and one, just one, jumped,
Folding her legs beneath her, and became
Suspended in my mind forevermore,
Hair streaming goodbye as she shot behind a martello tower.
Beside me a nun reading and a priest reading
And the feeling that there was an ending and beginning,
Here in all, somehow meeting;
That the eternal sea falling on the shore was all,
That the child still hung upon the air was all,
And the broom, burning in the late May sun was all, was all.

Walking To An Island

I.M. Barbara Callan

You can walk across to Omey
When the tide gives back the land,
Following the way across the sea-ribbed sand
Walking, not swimming to an island.

A butterfly trembles on the sea thrift,
The gulls caoin in the wind
And we sit where the sea meets the shore
On the edge of everything.

And there is no place here for mourning
For what will be will be,
And time will dance us all in the end
To some strand at the edge of the sea.

Here the ocean holds the last of the westering sun
A gem in the heel of her hand,
And now Omey has her own bright pearl
In the earth at the edge of the strand.

You Think It Is The Wind

You think it is the wind carousing round
The house, but it is not the wind
Raddling the thorn, the fuchsia and the
Tangled brambles in the ditch;

It is not the wind sending the
Turf smoke choking down the chimney's throat,
Knocking at the panes with invisible hands;

It is the voices of the dead, their whispers
And their shouts, they howl across the land,
Across the bay, the long dead and the newly dead.

And we should go into the night, and face
Into the wind, and in the haggard howl out loud against
Its flying fists its bullying roar, shouting
Until our lungs are fit to burst – not yet! not yet!

The Running Boys of Summer

Summer's end is marked here
Not by swallows, feathered crochets
On the wires bare clefs,
But by the solid lump of silence in the house.
The summer children left today
A single speckled alley on the rug
I find while putting toys away
A little green glass ball that tugs
And says, 'They're gone.'

The only sounds: the chimney wind
As I burn rubbish in the stove,
The empty fridge humming away
Electric idiot in the kitchen,
What does he know of love?
Outside there is nowt but mist and cloud, the day
Can't make his mind up what he's doing either.

I gather towels and bedding for
The wash – no boys are in the haggard
Kicking balls, no boys hang on the gate
Feeding the donkey carrots;
No boys clamour for the beach,
No boys shorewards to catch the crabs;
(Won't they be glad the Connemara crabs?
Free from the dangled rashers off the pier,
The hours in bucket prison 'till let free again.)

The sea is calm and flat today,
'Bofin coming and going in the mist,
No weather now to fret about;
I can sup my coffee in the town and linger on
No boys to ask, 'When can we go?'

But I would give all that I've got
To have them back all sleepy eyed
Over the breakfast, planning out the day;
Which bay to swim, which beach to dig,
Where to make the cricket pitch.

And the summer's end is marked now
Not by the swallows music on the wires,
But by the voices that are gone, no longer there,
The running boys of summer
Have taken to the air,
Yet I can feel and hear them everywhere.

The Sky Road

When they sorted out who would have what,
Gave some the grass and some rich loamy soil,
For growing sheep like wooly bombs and cattle fat as butter,
The Gods looked down on Connemara and one muttered,
'The poor devils, nowt but bog and stone and sea,
Hardly a tree that's worth its name.
The game's a bogie. We could try
To make it up to them by giving them
The lion's share of light and sky.'

And that is why somedays there seems to be
Nothing but sky here, a sky so big it dwarfs the land,
And why somedays the light
Would have you drunk with it.

And that is why somedays there is a soft and pastel sky,
So subtle that it smooths out rocks and sand and sea until
You can't tell where the sky ends, sea begins
Smudged into one pale pearl wall, big as the world.

And that is why a blush of cloud straggling across the Bens,
Looks like a lock of wool caught on a rusty wire,
Twitching in the wind.

And that is why at night sometimes the stars
Seem close enough for you to reach
And fill your pockets with them.

And that is why somedays clouds roll, creamy and fat,
Against a cobalt blue the colour of the Virgin's cloak
Looking not like a sky, but like a child's painting of a sky.

And that is why sunsets sometimes outdo
The paintbox: polished brass, rose hips,
Molten lava, candy floss and scarlet woman's lips,
Splashed across the burning curtains of the West.

And that is why they have a road here,
Bóthar na Spéire, The Sky Road,
That will take you, if you have a mind for it –
And can keep going just that extra country mile –
All the way up to the endless Connemara sky.

After

When I am gone into the stars,
When my steps no longer whisper
On the old stone flags before the house,
And my breath no longer clouds the cool night air
As I turn the key in the sleeping cottage door –
Come to this spot and sit and watch
Here, quietly on a day of high summer,
When a small, few clouds come softly from the west
And the earth is humming with the summers song;
Sit on this bank as I did when I came here first
And watch the combers race upon the strand.

No tears, no sighing, just remember how
A dream once brought me to this place,
And simply say,
'He used to like it here,
He used to like it here.'

Strange Lights Over Bexleyheath

Mike Harding
ISBN 978-1-906817-14-5 PBK £9.99

Do you remember how we though the world would end,
With spindly, giant, robot legs above Big Ben?
With Martian Crane flies, tower-block high, stalking
Above a boiling Thames...

In a post-apocalyptic world Glaswegian winos cross paths with ancient mermaidens in an innovative blend of fairy tale, science fiction and social realism. Though Harding's is an existential, fantasy world – be it a dystopian London, or the enchanted Oz – he invariably shows that only through the contemplation of the everyday can truth, the meaning and beauty be understood.

Strange Lights Over Bexleyheath is both a tribute to and a parody of the literary greats as well as being a provocative read in its own right.

Luath Press Limited

committed to publishing well written books worth reading

LUATH PRESS takes its name from Robert Burns, whose little collie Luath (Gael., swift or nimble) tripped up Jean Armour at a wedding and gave him the chance to speak to the woman who was to be his wife and the abiding love of his life. Burns called one of 'The Twa Dogs' Luath after Cuchullin's hunting dog in Ossian's *Fingal*. Luath Press was established in 1981 in the heart of Burns country, and now resides a few steps up the road from Burns' first lodgings on Edinburgh's Royal Mile.
Luath offers you distinctive writing with a hint of unexpected pleasures.

Most bookshops in the UK, the US, Canada, Australia, New Zealand and parts of Europe either carry our books in stock or can order them for you. To order direct from us, please send a £sterling cheque, postal order, international money order or your credit card details (number, address of cardholder and expiry date) to us at the address below. Please add post and packing as follows: UK – £1.00 per delivery address; overseas surface mail – £2.50 per delivery address; overseas airmail – £3.50 for the first book to each delivery address, plus £1.00 for each additional book by airmail to the same address. If your order is a gift, we will happily enclose your card or message at no extra charge.

ILLUSTRATION: IAN KELLAS

Luath Press Limited
543/2 Castlehill
The Royal Mile
Edinburgh EH1 2ND
Scotland
Telephone: 0131 225 4326 (24 hours)
Fax: 0131 225 4324
email: sales@luath.co.uk
Website: www.luath.co.uk